THE
EASTER
STORY

THE EASTER STORY

FROM THE GOSPELS

EDITED BY
MARGUERITE NORTHRUP

THE METROPOLITAN
MUSEUM OF ART

Distributed by New York Graphic Society, Greenwich, Connecticut

Grateful acknowledgment is made to The Reverend Canon Edward N. West, Th.D., Litt.D., Cathedral Church of St. John The Divine, for his invaluable assistance.

Designed by Peter Oldenburg. Composed in Bembo and Perpetua by Clarke & Way, Inc. Printed in an edition of 25,000 copies on Mohawk Superfine by Lebanon Valley Offset Company. Bound by J. F. Tapley Co.

For God so loved the world,
that he gave his only begotten Son,
that whosoever believeth in him
should not perish,
but have everlasting life.

JOHN 3:16

The Entry into Jerusalem

AND when they drew nigh unto Jerusalem, and were
come to Bethphage, unto the mount of Olives, then
sent Jesus two disciples, Saying unto them, Go into the
village over against you, and straightway ye shall find
an ass tied, and a colt with her: loose them, and bring
them unto me. And if any man say ought unto you, ye
shall say, The Lord hath need of them; and straightway

he will send them. . . . And the disciples went, and did as Jesus commanded them, And brought the ass, and the colt, and put on them their clothes, and they set him thereon. And a very great multitude spread their garments in the way; others cut down branches from the trees, and strawed them in the way. And the multitudes that went before, and that followed, cried, saying, Hosanna to the son of David: Blessed is he that cometh in the name of the Lord; Hosanna in the highest.

The Cleansing of the Temple

AND Jesus went into the temple of God, and cast out all them that sold and bought in the temple, and overthrew the tables of the moneychangers, and the seats of them that sold doves, And said unto them, It is written, My house shall be called the house of prayer; but ye have made it a den of thieves. And the blind and the lame came to him in the temple; and he healed them. And when the chief priests and scribes saw the wonderful things that he did, and the children crying in the temple, and saying, Hosanna to the son of David; they were sore displeased.

THEN one of the twelve, called Judas Iscariot, went unto the chief priests, And said unto them, What will ye give me, and I will deliver him unto you? And they covenanted with him for thirty pieces of silver. And from that time he sought opportunity to betray him.

The Last Supper

THEN came the day of unleavened bread, when the passover must be killed. And he sent Peter and John, saying, Go and prepare us the passover, that we may eat.

... And when the hour was come, he sat down, and the twelve apostles with him. And he said unto them, With desire I have desired to eat this passover with you before

I suffer: For I say unto you, I will not any more eat thereof, until it be fulfilled in the kingdom of God. And he took the cup, and gave thanks, and said, Take this, and divide it among yourselves: For I say unto you, I will not drink of the fruit of the vine, until the kingdom of God shall come. And he took bread, and gave thanks, and brake it, and gave unto them, saying, This is my body which is given for you: this do in remembrance of me. Likewise also the cup after supper, saying, This cup is the new testament in my blood, which is shed for you. But, behold, the hand of him that betrayeth me is with me on the table.

The Maundy

JESUS knowing that the Father had given all things into his hands, and that he was come from God, and went to God; He riseth from supper, and laid aside his garments; and took a towel, and girded himself. After that he poureth water into a bason, and began to wash the disciples' feet, and to wipe them with the towel wherewith he was girded. . . . So after he had washed their feet, and had taken his garments, and was set down again, he said unto them, Know ye what I have done to you? Ye call me Master and Lord: and ye say well; for so I am. If I then, your Lord and Master, have washed your feet; ye also ought to wash one another's feet. For I have given you an example, that ye should do as I have done to you. Verily, verily, I say unto you, The servant is not greater than his lord; neither he that is sent greater than he that sent him. . . . A new commandment I give unto you, That ye love one another; as I have loved you, that ye also love one another.

The Agony in the Garden

AND he came out, and went, as he was wont, to the mount of Olives; and his disciples also followed him. And when he was at the place, he said unto them, Pray

that ye enter not into temptation. And he was withdrawn
from them about a stone's cast, and kneeled down, and
prayed, Saying, Father, if thou be willing, remove this
cup from me: nevertheless not my will, but thine, be
done. And there appeared an angel unto him from

heaven, strengthening him. And being in an agony he
prayed more earnestly: and his sweat was as it were
great drops of blood falling down to the ground. And
when he rose up from prayer, and was come to his
disciples, he found them sleeping for sorrow, And said
unto them, Why sleep ye? rise and pray, lest ye enter
into temptation.

omine ad adiu
uandium me festia.
Gloria pñ et filio
et spiritui sancto

Sicut erat in prin
cipio et nunc et sem
per et in secula seculo
rum. amen. Inuitat.

The Betrayal and Arrest

AND while he yet spake, lo, Judas, one of the twelve, came, and with him a great multitude with swords and staves, from the chief priests and elders of the people. Now he that betrayed him gave them a sign, saying, Whomsoever I shall kiss, that same is he: hold him fast. And forthwith he came to Jesus, and said, Hail, master; and kissed him. And Jesus said unto him, Friend, wherefore art thou come? Then came they, and laid hands on Jesus, and took him. And, behold, one of them which were with Jesus stretched out his hand, and drew his sword, and struck a servant of the high priest's, and smote off his ear. Then said Jesus unto him, Put up again thy sword into his place: for all they that take the sword shall perish with the sword. . . . But all this was done, that the scriptures of the prophets might be fulfilled. Then all the disciples forsook him, and fled.

Peter's Denials

THEN took they him, and led him, and brought him into the high priest's house. And Peter followed afar off. And when they had kindled a fire in the midst of the hall, and were set down together, Peter sat down among them. But a certain maid beheld him as he sat by the fire, and earnestly looked upon him, and said, This man was also with him. And he denied him, saying, Woman, I know him not. And after a little while another saw him, and said, Thou art also of them. And Peter said, Man, I am not. And about the space of one hour after another confidently affirmed, saying, Of a truth this fellow also was with him: for he is a Galilaean. And Peter said, Man, I know not what thou sayest. And immediately, while he yet spake, the cock crew. And the Lord turned, and looked upon Peter. And Peter remembered the word of the Lord, how he had said unto him, Before the cock crow, thou shalt deny me thrice. And Peter went out, and wept bitterly.

Christ before Caiaphas

AND the chief priests and all the council sought for witness against Jesus to put him to death; and found none. For many bare false witness against him, but their witness agreed not together. And there arose certain, and bare false witness against him, saying, We heard him say, I will destroy this temple that is made with hands, and within three days I will build another made without hands. But neither so did their witness agree together.

And the high priest stood up in the midst, and asked Jesus, saying, Answerest thou nothing? what is it which these witness against thee? But he held his peace, and answered nothing. Again the high priest asked him, and said unto him, Art thou the Christ, the Son of the Blessed? And Jesus said, I am: and ye shall see the Son of man sitting on the right hand of power, and coming in the clouds of heaven. Then the high priest rent his clothes, and saith, What need we any further witnesses? Ye have heard the blasphemy: what think ye? And they all condemned him to be guilty of death.

Christic before Pilate

Tʜᴇɴ led they Jesus from Caiaphas unto the hall of judgment. . . . Pilate then went out unto them, and said, What accusation bring ye against this man? They

answered and said unto him, If he were not a malefactor, we would not have delivered him up unto thee. . . . Then Pilate entered into the judgment hall again, and called

Jesus, and said unto him, Art thou the King of the Jews? . . . Jesus answered, My kingdom is not of this world. . . . Pilate therefore said unto him, Art thou a king then? Jesus answered, Thou sayest that I am a king. To this end was I born, and for this cause came I into the world, that I should bear witness unto the truth. . . . Pilate saith unto him, What is truth? And when he had said this, he went out again unto the Jews, and saith unto them, I find in him no fault at all. But ye have a custom, that I should release unto you one at the passover: will ye therefore that I release unto you the King of the Jews? Then cried they all again, saying, Not this man, but Barabbas. Now Barabbas was a robber.

Ecce Homo

THEN Pilate therefore took Jesus, and scourged him. And the soldiers platted a crown of thorns, and put it on his head, and they put on him a purple robe, And said, Hail, King of the Jews! and they smote him with their hands. Pilate therefore went forth again, and saith unto them, Behold, I bring him forth to you, that ye may know that I find no fault in him. Then came Jesus forth, wearing the crown of thorns, and the purple robe. And Pilate saith unto them, Behold the man! When the chief priests therefore and officers saw him, they cried out, saying, Crucify him, crucify him. Pilate saith unto them, Take ye him, and crucify him: for I find no fault in him. The Jews answered him, We have a law, and by our law he ought to die, because he made himself the Son of God. When Pilate therefore heard that saying, he

was the more afraid; And went again into the judgment hall, and saith unto Jesus, Whence art thou? But Jesus gave him no answer. Then saith Pilate unto him, Speakest thou not unto me? knowest thou not that I have power to crucify thee, and have power to release thee? Jesus answered, Thou couldest have no power at all against me, except it were given thee from above: therefore he that delivered me unto thee hath the greater sin. And from thenceforth Pilate sought to release him. . . . But they cried out, Away with him, away with him, crucify him. Pilate saith unto them, Shall I crucify your King? The chief priests answered, We have no king but Caesar. Then delivered he him therefore unto them to be crucified.

The Way of the Cross

AND as they led him away, they laid hold upon one Simon, a Cyrenian, coming out of the country, and on him they laid the cross, that he might bear it after Jesus. And there followed him a great company of people, and of women, which also bewailed and lamented him. But Jesus turning unto them said, Daughters of Jerusalem, weep not for me, but weep for yourselves, and for your children.

The Crucifixion

AND when they were come to the place, which is called Calvary, there they crucified him, and the malefactors, one on the right hand, and the other on the

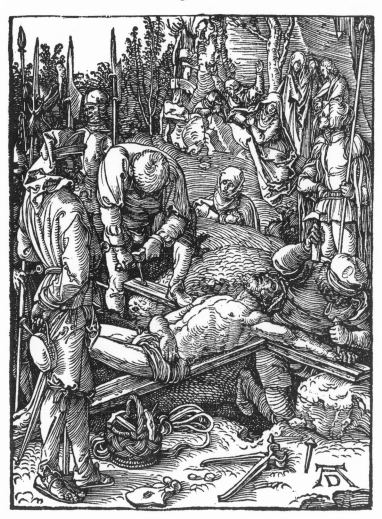

left. Then said Jesus, Father, forgive them; for they know not what they do. And they parted his raiment, and cast lots. And the people stood beholding. And the rulers also with them derided him, saying, He saved others; let him save himself, if he be Christ, the chosen of God. . . . And a superscription also was written over him in letters of Greek, and Latin, and Hebrew, THIS IS THE KING OF THE JEWS. And one of the malefactors which were hanged railed on him, saying, If thou be Christ, save thyself and us. But the other answering rebuked him, saying, Dost not thou fear God, seeing thou art in the same condemnation? And we indeed justly; for we receive the due reward of our deeds: but this man hath done nothing amiss. And he said unto Jesus, Lord, remember me when thou comest into thy kingdom. And Jesus said unto him, Verily I say unto thee, To day shalt thou be with me in paradise.

Now there stood by the cross of Jesus his mother, and his mother's sister, Mary the wife of Cleophas, and Mary Magdalene. When Jesus therefore saw his mother, and the disciple standing by, whom he loved, he saith unto his mother, Woman, behold thy son! Then saith he to the disciple, Behold thy mother! And from that hour that disciple took her unto his own home.

And they that passed by railed on him, wagging their heads, and saying, Ah, thou that destroyest the temple, and buildest it in three days, Save thyself, and come down from the cross. Likewise also the chief priests mocking said among themselves with the scribes, He saved others; himself he cannot save. . . . And when the

Sicut erat in principio et nunc et semper et in secula seculorum. Amen. ps̄m.

Beata xp̄isti
passio sit n̄ra
liberacio et per hanc
nobis gaudia para

sixth hour was come, there was darkness over the whole land until the ninth hour. And at the ninth hour Jesus cried with a loud voice, saying, Eloi, Eloi, lama sabachthani? which is, being interpreted, My God, my God, why hast thou forsaken me? And some of them that stood by, when they heard it, said, Behold, he calleth Elias.

AFTER this, Jesus knowing that all things were now accomplished, that the scripture might be fulfilled, saith, I thirst. Now there was set a vessel full of vinegar: and they filled a spunge with vinegar, and put it upon hyssop, and put it to his mouth. When Jesus therefore had received the vinegar, he said, It is finished.

AND when Jesus had cried with a loud voice, he said, Father, into thy hands I commend my spirit: and having said thus, he gave up the ghost.

AND, behold, the veil of the temple was rent in twain from the top to the bottom; and the earth did quake, and the rocks rent; And the graves were opened; and many bodies of the saints which slept arose. . . . Now when the centurion, and they that were with him, watching Jesus, saw the earthquake, and those things that were done, they feared greatly, saying, Truly this was the Son of God.

THE Jews therefore, because it was the preparation, that the bodies should not remain upon the cross on the sabbath day, (for that sabbath day was an high day,) besought Pilate that their legs might be broken, and that they might be taken away. Then came the soldiers, and brake the legs of the first, and of the other which was crucified with him. But when they came to Jesus, and saw that he was dead already, they brake not his legs: But one of the soldiers with a spear pierced his side, and forthwith came there out blood and water. And he that saw it bare record, and his record is true.

The Descent from the Cross

AND now when the even was come, because it was the preparation, that is, the day before the sabbath, Joseph of Arimathaea, an honourable counsellor, which also waited for the kingdom of God, came, and went in boldly unto Pilate, and craved the body of Jesus. And Pilate marvelled if he were already dead: and calling unto him the centurion, he asked him whether he had been any while dead. And when he knew it of the centurion, he gave the body to Joseph. And he bought fine linen, and took him down, and wrapped him in the linen, and laid him in a sepulchre which was hewn out of a rock, and rolled a stone unto the door of the sepulchre. And Mary Magdalene and Mary the mother of Joses beheld where he was laid.

The Resurrection

IN the end of the sabbath, as it began to dawn toward the first day of the week, came Mary Magdalene and the other Mary to see the sepulchre. And, behold, there was a great earthquake: for the angel of the Lord descended from heaven, and came and rolled back the stone from the door, and sat upon it. His countenance was like lightning, and his raiment white as snow: And for fear of him the keepers did shake, and became as dead men. And the angel answered and said unto the women, Fear not ye: for I know that ye seek Jesus, which was crucified. He is not here: for he is risen, as he said. Come, see the place where the Lord lay. And go quickly, and tell his disciples that he is risen from the dead; and, behold, he goeth before you into Galilee; there shall ye see him:

lo, I have told you. And they departed quickly from the sepulchre with fear and great joy; and did run to bring his disciples word.

B<small>UT</small> Mary stood without at the sepulchre weeping: and as she wept, she stooped down, and looked into the sepulchre, And seeth two angels in white sitting, the one at the head, and the other at the feet, where the body of Jesus had lain. And they say unto her, Woman, why weepest thou? She saith unto them, Because they have

taken away my Lord, and I know not where they have
laid him. And when she had thus said, she turned herself
back, and saw Jesus standing, and knew not that it was
Jesus. Jesus saith unto her, Woman, why weepest thou?
whom seekest thou? She, supposing him to be the gard-
ener, saith unto him, Sir, if thou have borne him hence,
tell me where thou hast laid him, and I will take him
away. Jesus saith unto her, Mary. She turned herself, and
saith unto him, Rabboni; which is to say, Master. Jesus
saith unto her, Touch me not; for I am not yet ascended

to my Father: but go to my brethren, and say unto them, I ascend unto my Father, and your Father; and to my God, and your God.

Emmaus

AND, behold, two of them went that same day to a village called Emmaus, which was from Jerusalem about threescore furlongs. And they talked together of all these things which had happened. And it came to pass, that, while they communed together and reasoned, Jesus himself drew near, and went with them. But their eyes were holden that they should not know him. . . . And it came to pass, as he sat at meat with them, he took bread, and blessed it, and brake, and gave to them. And their eyes were opened, and they knew him; and he vanished out of their sight. . . . And they rose up the same hour, and returned to Jerusalem, and found the eleven gathered together, and them that were with them, Saying, The Lord is risen indeed, and hath appeared to Simon. . . . And as they thus spake, Jesus himself stood in the midst of them, and saith unto them, Peace be unto you.

"My Lord and my God"

BUT Thomas, one of the twelve, called Didymus, was not with them when Jesus came. The other disciples therefore said unto him, We have seen the Lord. But he said unto them, Except I shall see in his hands the print of the nails, and put my finger into the print of the nails, and thrust my hand into his side, I will not believe. And after

eight days again his disciples were within, and Thomas with them: then came Jesus, the doors being shut, and stood in the midst, and said, Peace be unto you. Then saith he to Thomas, Reach hither thy finger, and behold my hands; and reach hither thy hand, and thrust it into my side: and be not faithless, but believing. And Thomas answered and said unto him, My Lord and my God. Jesus saith unto him, Thomas, because thou hast seen me, thou hast believed: blessed are they that have not seen, and yet have believed.

TEXTS

The selections from the Gospels are from the King James Version of the Bible.

The Entry into Jerusalem
Matthew 21:1–3, 6–9

The Cleansing of the Temple
Matthew 21:12–15; 26:14–16

The Last Supper
Luke 22:7–8, 14–21

The Maundy
John 13:3–5, 12–16, 34

The Agony in the Garden
Luke 22:39–46

The Betrayal and Arrest
Matthew 26:47–52, 56

Peter's Denials
Luke 22:54–62

Christ before Caiaphas
Mark 14:55–64

Christ before Pilate
John 18:28a, 29–30, 33, 36, 37a, b

Ecce Homo
John 19:1–12a, 15–16a

The Way of the Cross
Luke 23:26–28

The Crucifixion
Luke 23:33–35, 38–43; John 19:25–27; Mark 15:29–31, 33–35; John 19:28–30; Luke 23:46; Matthew 27:51–52, 54; John 19:31–35

The Descent from the Cross
Mark 15:42–47

The Resurrection
Matthew 28:1–8; John 20:11–17

Emmaus
Luke 24:13–16, 30–31, 33–34, 36

"My Lord and my God"
John 20:24–29

ILLUSTRATIONS

Unless otherwise noted, the works are reproduced facsimile size.

Frontispiece Rembrandt Harmensz. van Ryn (Dutch, 1606–1669). Oil on canvas, 18⅝ × 14⅝ inches, about 1660. The Mr. and Mrs. Isaac D. Fletcher Collection. Bequest of Isaac D. Fletcher, 17.120.222

7, 10, 12, 17, 18, 24, 34, 35, 38 Albrecht Dürer (German, 1471–1528). Woodcuts, from the Small Passion, about 1509–1511. Gift of Junius S. Morgan, 19.73.176, 178, 179, 183, 185, 193, 199, 201, 203

9 Rembrandt. Etching, dated 1635 (second state). Gift of Felix M. Warburg and his family, 41.1.49

13 Rembrandt. Etching, about 1657. Harris Brisbane Dick Fund, 23.16.1

14, 28 Pages from the Belles Heures of the Duke of Berry, illuminated by the Limbourg brothers. Franco-Netherlandish, about 1410–1413. The Cloisters Collection, 54.1.1

20–21 Rembrandt. Etching, 13¾ × 17¹⁵⁄₁₆ inches, dated 1655 (seventh state). Gift of Felix M. Warburg and his family, 41.1.36

23 Unknown Flemish painter (second half of the fifteenth century). Tempera and oil on wood, 42⅜ × 32⅜ inches. Bequest of George D. Pratt, 43.95

26–27 Rembrandt. Etching, 15³⁄₁₆ × 17¹⁵⁄₁₆ inches, dated 1653 (third state). Gift of Felix M. Warburg and his family, 41.1.32

31 Hubert van Eyck (Flemish, died 1426). Tempera and oil on canvas, transferred from wood, 22¼ × 7¾ inches. Fletcher Fund, 33.92

32 Rembrandt, Etching, dated 1654. Gift of Felix M. Warburg, 17.14

37 Rembrandt. Etching, dated 1654 (first state). Gift of Felix M. Warburg and his family, 41.1.58

40